LAUGH OUT LOUD!

THE ANIMAL ANTICS JOKE BOOK

Sean Connolly and Kay Barnham

W
FRANKLIN WATTS
LONDON • SYDNEY

Essex County Council
3013020321343 3

First published in 2012 by Franklin Watts

Copyright © 2012 Arcturus Publishing Limited

Franklin Watts
338 Euston Road
London
NW1 3BH

Franklin Watts Australia
Level 17/207 Kent Street, Sydney, NSW 2000

Produced by Arcturus Publishing Limited,
26/27 Bickels Yard, 151–153 Bermondsey Street, London SE1 3HA

All rights reserved.

Editor: Joe Harris
Illustrations: Adam Clay
Layout Design: Notion Design

A CIP catalogue record for this book is available from the British Library.

Dewey Decimal Classification Number: 818.6'02-dc23

ISBN: 978 1 4451 1490 3

Franklin Watts is a division of Hachette Children's Books, an Hachette UK company.
www.hachette.co.uk

Printed in China

SL001836EN
Supplier 03, Date 0512, Print Run 1962

CONTENTS

Why are dogs such bad dancers?
They have two left feet.

What's worse than raining cats and dogs?
Hailing taxis.

What happened to the cat that swallowed a ball of wool?
She had mittens.

How can you keep a wet dog from smelling?
Hold its nose.

Have you put some more water in the goldfish bowl?
No. It still hasn't drunk the water I put in when I first bought it!

Hey, you can't fish here, this is a private lake!
I'm not fishing, I'm teaching my pet worm to swim!

How do fleas get from one animal to another?
They itch hike!

What's the special offer at the pet shop this week?
Buy one cat – get one flea!

What do you call a multistorey pigpen?
A styscraper.

Why did the dog wear gloves?
Because it was a boxer.

My dog's a blacksmith.
How can you tell?
When I tell him off, he makes a bolt for the door.

Why did it take the Dalmatian so long to choose a holiday?
He was looking for just the right spot.

Why was the cat scared of the tree?
Because of its bark.

What animal wears a long coat in the winter and pants in the summer?
A dog!

What is a good pet for small children?
A rattlesnake!

What type of dog can tell the time?
A watchdog.

How do you spell mouse trap using only 3 letters?
C A T!

Which pets are the noisiest?
Trumpets!

What did the dog say when it sat on some sandpaper?
Ruff!

Classified ad in local paper:
'Dog free to good home – eats anything. Loves children!'

How do you stop a dog from barking in the back seat of a car?
Put it in the front seat.

What are dog biscuits made from?
Collie-flour!

Johnny: Mum, is our dog metric?
Mum: Why do you ask?
Johnny: Because Dad said it has just had a litre of puppies!

Why did the dog limp into the Wild West saloon?
He came to find the cowboy who shot his paw!

I think I'm turning into a young cat.
You must be kitten me!

What do you call a cat that chases outlaws?
A posse cat!

What do you get if you cross an insect and a rabbit?
Bugs Bunny.

Did you hear about the well-behaved cat?
It was purrfect.

One boy says to another boy, 'My pet's called Tiny.'
'Why?' asks his friend.
'Because he's my newt.'

Knock, knock!
Who's there?
Alf.
Alf who?
Alf feed the cat while you're on holiday!

What do cats drink in the desert?
Evaporated milk.

What do you call a column topped with a statue of a famous cat?
A caterpillar!

What do you call a cat with eight legs?
An octopus.

What do you call a woman with a cat on her head?
Kitty.

What did the dog say when his owner stopped him from chewing the newspaper?
'You took the words out of my mouth!'

What do you get if you drop birdseed in your shoes?
Pigeon toes.

What did the clean dog say to the dirty dog?
Long time no flea!

My dog is a real problem. He chases anything and everything on a bike. I don't know what to do.
Just take his bike away!

Which cats are great at bowling?
Alley cats.

What sort of dog is good at looking after children?
A baby setter.

Doctor, I think I'm a cat!
How long have you felt like this?
Since I was a kitten!

What do you get if a cat sits on a beach at Christmas?
Sandy claws!

First cat: Where do fleas go in the winter?
Second cat: Search me!

What happened to the Scottish cat that ran into the road without looking?
It was kilt!

How do you find a lost dog?
Make a sound like a bone!

Teacher: Can you define 'dogmatic'?
Pupil: Is it a robot pet?

Did you hear about the cat that sucked a lemon?
He was a sourpuss.

What's a horse's favourite sport?
Stable tennis.

What's the difference between a well-dressed gentleman and an exhausted dog?
One wears an expensive suit and the other just pants.

Doctor, I feel as sick as a dog.
I'll make an appointment for you to see a vet!

Mum: Did you put the cat out?
Kid: I didn't need to. It wasn't on fire!

What do you use to clean a cat's hair?
A catacomb.

What do you give a sick parakeet?
Tweetment!

Why was the pig covered in ink?
Because it lived in a pen.

Why do pigs make terrible drivers?
They're all road hogs.

How do you make a cat happy?
Send it to the Canary Islands!

What do you call the place where cats and dogs go to get new tails?
A retailer!

What do you call a dog that is always rushing around?
A dash-hound!

Where do you buy baby birds?
At the chickout.

What do you get if you leave a parrot cage open?
A polygon.

What do you get if you cross a honeydew and a sheepdog?
A melon collie.

Doctor, I think I'm a dog.
Well, take a seat and I'll have a look at you.
I can't – I'm not allowed on the furniture!

Did you hear about the boy who spilled spot remover on his dog?
The dog vanished.

Why did the chicken sit on an axe?
She wanted to hatchet.

What did the traffic warden put on the car outside the dog kennel?
A barking ticket.

What's a dog's favourite hobby?
Collecting fleas.

What does your pet snake become if he gets a government job?
A civil serpent!

Why did the cat say 'woof'?
It was learning a foreign language.

What do you get when you cross a parrot and a cat?
A carrot!

Where do huskies train for dogsled races?
In the mushroom.

Why did the dogs jump in the lake?
To catch a catfish.

What type of pet just lies around doing nothing?
A carpet.

Why did the dog chase his own tail?
He was trying to make ends meet.

Which dog wears a white coat and looks through microscopes?
A lab!

What do you call a prisoner's parakeet?
A jail bird!

Why did the cat pounce on the computer?
Because he saw a mouse.

What's happening when you hear 'Meow – splat! Woof – splat!'
It's raining cats and dogs.

What has more lives than a cat?
A frog – it croaks every night.

Did you hear about the cat who drank three saucers of water in one go?
She wanted to set a new lap record!

Doctor, I feel like a dog!
Sit!

Why do dogs wag their tails?
Because no one else will do it for them.

What's red and green and jumps out of planes?
A parrot-trooper!

Why did the Dalmatian go to the eye doctor?
He was seeing spots.

What did Shakespeare's cat say?
'Tabby or not tabby...'

Why do dogs run in circles?
Because it's hard to run in squares.

What do you get when you cross a dog with a sheep?
A sheep that can round itself up.

What did the cowboy say when the bear ate his hunting hound?
Doggone!

What do parakeets wear to the beach?
Beakinis.

What happens when cats fight?
They hiss and make up.

What do you call rabbits marching backward?
A receding hare-line.

Why do terriers make great fighter pilots?
Because they're good in a dogfight.

Why did the girl oil her pet mouse?
Because it squeaked.

What did the bunny say to the carrot?
It's been nice gnawing you.

What do you use to comb a rabbit?
A hare-brush.

What's more astounding than a talking dog?
A spelling bee.

What do you say to a dog before he eats?
'Bone appetit!'

What do you call a cat that does tricks?
A magic kit.

What do you call an Alsatian in jeans and a T-shirt?
A plain-clothes police dog.

What did the canary say when its new cage fell apart?
'Cheep! Cheep!'

What do you call a guard dog with a cold?
A germy shepherd.

How does a cat sing the musical scale?
Do-re-meow.

What do you call a hamster that can pick up an elephant?
Sir!

What does a cat say when he gets hurt?
Mee-OW!

How did the puppy stop the DVD player?
He used paws.

What do you get when you cross a dog with an elephant?
A really nervous postman.

Why are dogs longer at night than during the day?
Because they are let out in the evening and taken in in the morning.

What happens if you mix a bird, a car and a dog?
A flying carpet.

What kind of cat keeps the grass short?
A lawn meower.

Cat bumper sticker:
'Life is hard – then you nap.'

What kind of bird does construction work?
A crane.

Did you hear about the pig who walked around the world?
He was a globetrotter.

Why is it called a 'litter' of puppies?
Because they mess up the whole house.

What happened when the dog went to the flea circus?
He stole the show!

What did one flea say to the other flea?
'Should we walk or take the dog?'

Which birds steal from the bathroom?
Robber ducks.

What do you get when you cross a parrot with a pig?
An animal that hogs the conversation.

What do cats use to make coffee?
A purr-colator.

Which cat led the Chinese revolution?
Chairman Meow.

What do lazy dogs do for fun?
They chase parked cars.

Why did the tortoise cross the road?
To get to the Shell garage.

Why do birds lay eggs?
Because if they dropped them, they'd break.

What do you call a parakeet that plays ice hockey?
A cheep skate.

Where do young dogs sleep when they camp out?
In pup tents.

What do you call a vet with a sore throat?
A hoarse doctor.

When is it unlucky to see a white cat?
When you're a mouse.

Why don't you need a licence for a cat?
Because cats can't drive!

What do you give a pony with a sore throat?
Cough stirrup.

Who always succeeds?
A parakeet with no teeth.

Why was the toucan kicked out of the hotel?
Because he had an enormous bill!

What do you call a cat that has just eaten a whole duck?
A duck-filled fatty puss!

Teacher: Some plant names begin with the word 'dog'. Think of dogwood and dog rose. Can anyone think of another beginning with dog?
Pupil: Collie-flower!

Why did the teenage pig have to tidy her room?
Her mum said it looked like a pigsty.

Can a cat play patty-cake?
Paw-sibly.

What's it called when a dog does a TV commercial?
Ad-fur-tisement.

What do you call a Scottish parrot?
A macaw!

Which breed of dog can jump higher than a tree?
Any breed – trees can't jump!

What do you get if you cross a dog with a cheetah?
A dog that chases cars – and catches them!

In which month do dogs bark the least?
In February – it's the shortest month!

How did the little Scottish dog feel when he saw the monster?
Terrier-fied.

Glossary

blacksmith someone who makes and repairs metal objects

catacomb an underground place where dead bodies are buried

dogmatic stubborn about your ideas

evaporate to turn a liquid to vapour, especially when it is heated

saloon a place where people in the Wild West bought alcoholic drinks

Further Reading

Chatterton, Martin. *What a Hoot!* Kingfisher, 2005.

Dahl, Michael. *Roaring with Laughter*. Picture Window Books, 2004.

Winter, Judy A. *Jokes About Animals*. Capstone Press, 2010.

Index

Websites

CBBC 'Crack a Joke' game:
www.bbc.co.uk/cbbc/shows/cbbc-jokes

Yahoo! Kids Jokes:
http://kids.yahoo.com/jokes